THE DAILY LIFE MAYAN FAMILY

History for Kids
Children's History Books

BABY PROFESSOR
EDUCATION KIDS

Speedy Publishing LLC
40 E. Main St. #1156
Newark, DE 19711
www.speedypublishing.com
Copyright 2017

The Mayan culture was dominant in southern Mexico and Central America for hundreds of years. How did people live in the Mayan world? Let's find out.

THE MAYAN WORLD

The first Mayan communities developed along the Pacific coast of Central America and southern Mexico as early as 1800 BCE. The culture, and its kingdom of cooperating city-states, gradually expanded. Before 250 CE, there were large cities as well as ritual centers like Tikal and Calakmul.

TIKAL RUIN

MEXICAN MAN WORKING ON HIS HANDCRAFT

The Mayan culture continues today, but of course in the last hundred years much has changed. Let's look at daily life as it was for thousands of years, before gunpowder and gasoline and the Internet.

The Mayan world was divided into three classes:

- The nobility
- The middle class of artisans and merchants
- Everybody else

THE NOBILITY

The Mayan nobility was the smallest class in society. The nobles had most of the wealth and power. You almost always had to be born into one of the noble families to be part of the nobility.

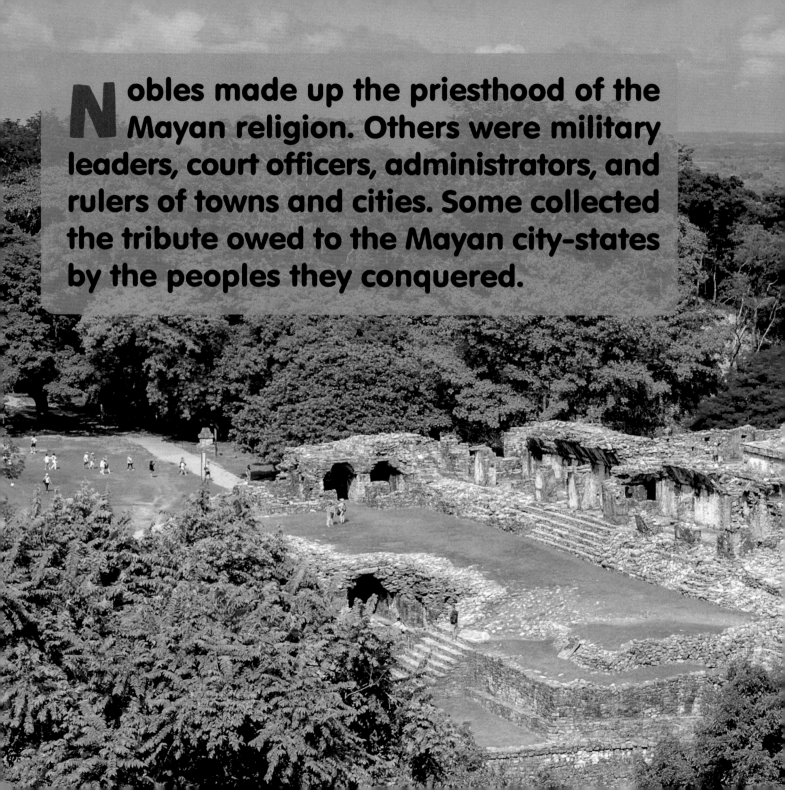

Nobles made up the priesthood of the Mayan religion. Others were military leaders, court officers, administrators, and rulers of towns and cities. Some collected the tribute owed to the Mayan city-states by the peoples they conquered.

MAYA CIVILIZATION

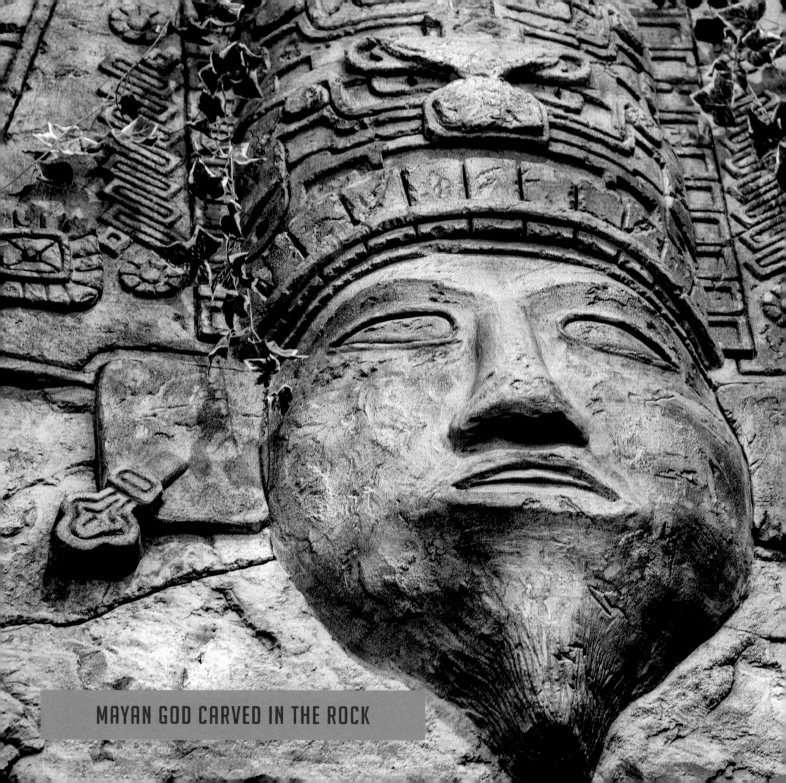

MAYAN GOD CARVED IN THE ROCK

In the Mayan belief system, the nobles spoke to the gods on behalf of the people, and told the people what the gods said and wanted. In the mind of many people, the nobles were in some way part-gods.

MAYAN RUINS

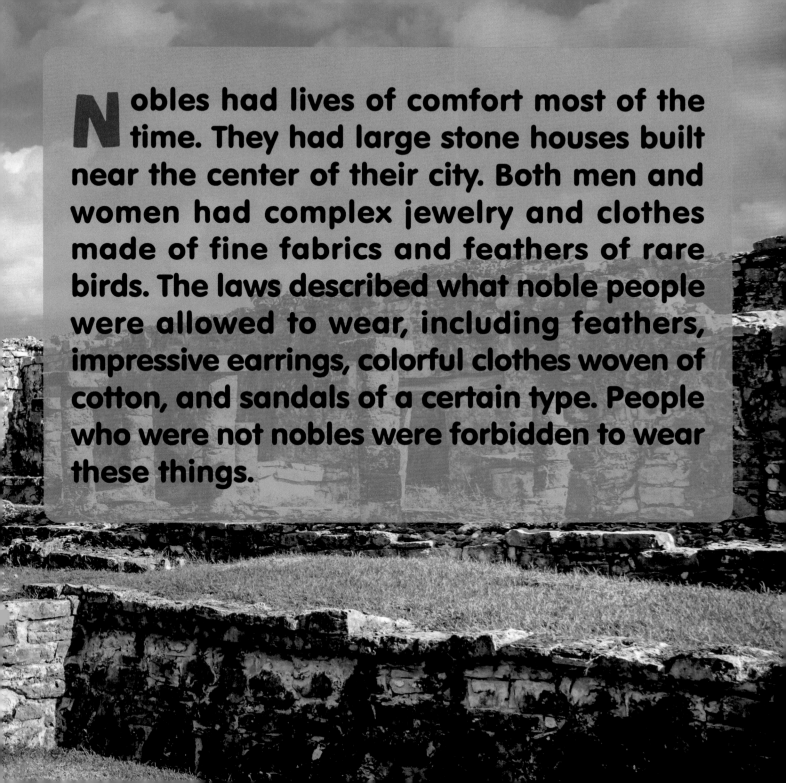

Nobles had lives of comfort most of the time. They had large stone houses built near the center of their city. Both men and women had complex jewelry and clothes made of fine fabrics and feathers of rare birds. The laws described what noble people were allowed to wear, including feathers, impressive earrings, colorful clothes woven of cotton, and sandals of a certain type. People who were not nobles were forbidden to wear these things.

Mayan nobles probably ate more meat than the people of the other classes, but in other ways their diet was pretty much the same. However, only Mayan nobles could afford to drink frothy chocolate drinks every day.

ANCIENT MAYAN STRUCTURES

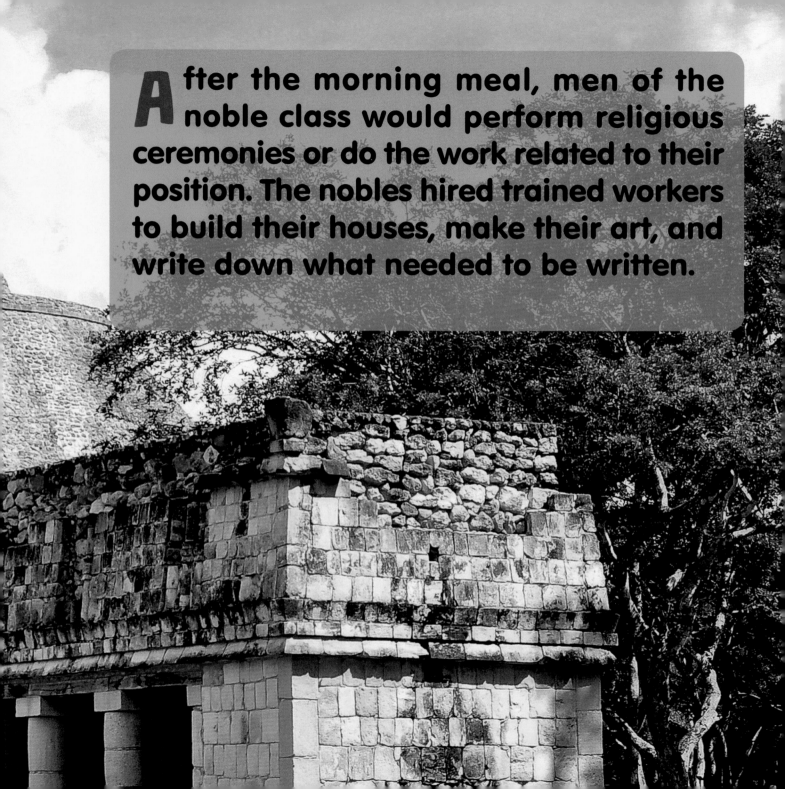

After the morning meal, men of the noble class would perform religious ceremonies or do the work related to their position. The nobles hired trained workers to build their houses, make their art, and write down what needed to be written.

On the other hand, the nobility had tasks as the people who spoke with the gods. As part of that conversation they had to offer their own blood. Normally they did not have to sacrifice their lives, but they had to jab themselves and bleed a significant amount of blood for use in religious ceremonies. The nobles considered this giving of blood a high honor, and often entered a sort of trance-like state while it was happening. Emerging from that state, they would report what they had learned from the gods.

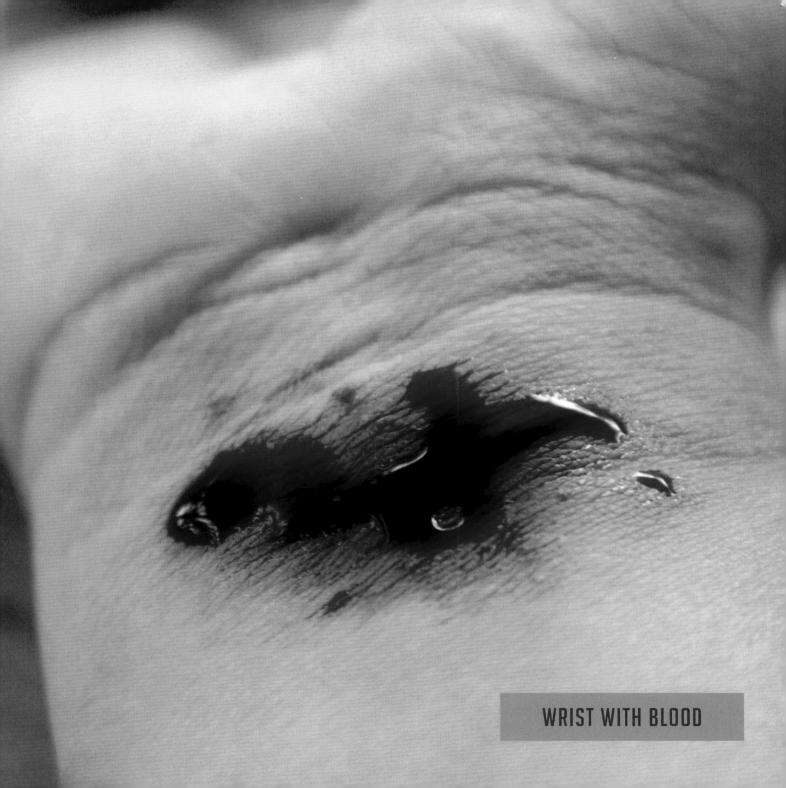

WRIST WITH BLOOD

ANCIENT MAYAN RITUAL DAGGER

The other tough part of being a noble is what might happen if your city-state lost a war with another Mayan city-state, or with another culture. Captured nobles were usually sacrificed to the gods of the winning side, often in painful public rituals.

THE ARTISANS

The artisans of the Mayan culture could come from noble or common families. They earned their position through the excellence of their work. Artisans created lovely works in stone, jewelry, fabric, and pottery. They made headdresses and robes from the colorful feathers of rare birds. The level of technical skill and artistic sense the surviving works demonstrate is very high.

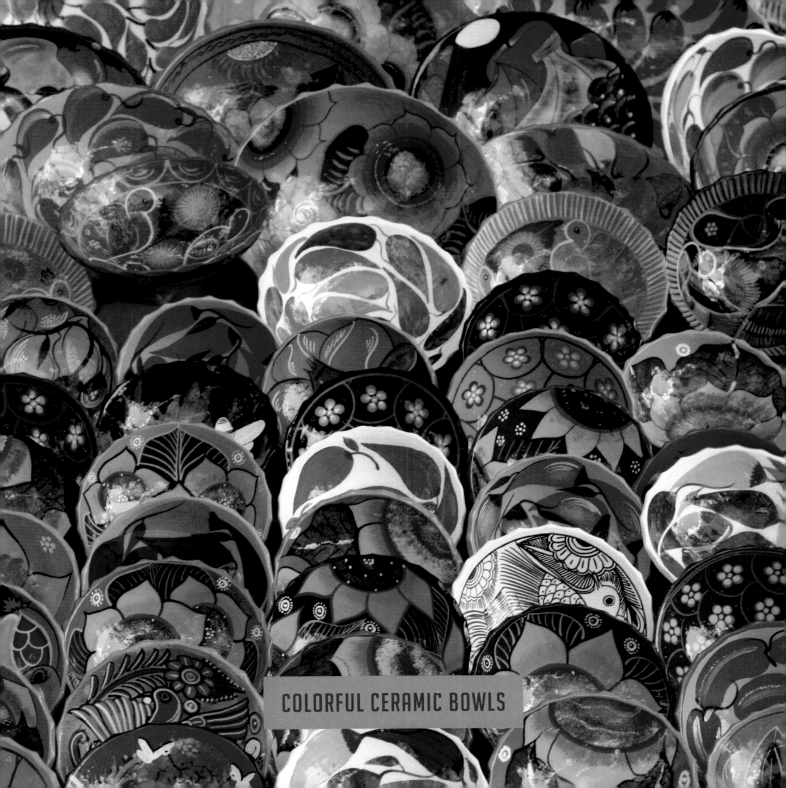

COLORFUL CERAMIC BOWLS

WEAVING REED MAT

The homes of craftsmen and artisans were smaller than those of the nobles, but much larger than those of everyday laborers. However, like the farmers and other workers, the artisans slept on reed mats in the one main room of the home.

Everybody got up early and started the day with family prayers. Then there was a breakfast, usually of a cooked cereal called "saka". On special days there would be a cup of hot chocolate.

HOT CHOCOLATE

ANCIENT MAYA STATUE

Many artisans worked in a room in their home, but others went off for the day to wherever they worked. This was especially true, of course, for builders, stonemasons, and people making large stone statues.

Those making jewelry or clothing involving feathers would have to go to dealers or to the market to find their supplies.

Artisans sold most of what they made to the nobility, but they also made goods to sell to anybody who wanted to buy them in the city market. They had to pay a tax on their sales, but the rest of the money helped pay for a comfortable life for their extended families (children, uncles and aunts, relatives of all sorts, and many servants).

HANDMADE TORTILLAS

At the end of the work day, the artisans and their families would gather for the main meal of the day. The meal might include tortillas, cooked meat, and fruit. People did not stay up late after the sun went down on the day.

EVERYBODY ELSE

Most of the Maya were commoners and spent every day doing hard work. The work might involve helping build a temple, or working on an irrigation ditch to bring water to fields, planting or tending crops.

IRRIGATION DITCH

ANCIENT STONE TOOL

The Mayans did not have a lot of complicated tools, and almost everything they did relied on muscle power. They did not have horses or oxen to help them with farm tasks like plowing, and they did not have metal with which to make farm tools, much less weapons. They did have sharp-edged stone tools, but keeping the edges sharp took work each day.

Women worked in their homes, which were made of woven sticks covered with mud. The women ground corn and cooked meals, raised the children, grew crops in gardens near their houses, gathered honey from beehives, and wove cloth. They used the cloth to make what the family wore, and what the family did not need they could sell in the market.

MAYAN HOME

TURKEYS AND HEN

Men, and boys who were old enough, worked in the fields during the growing season. Families might have dogs, and farmyard birds like ducks and turkeys that they kept for their eggs. Meat came from deer and wild pig which the men hunted, and from fish caught from the lakes and the ocean.

The commoners would be called away from the farm in times of need to help haul heavy loads, serve the nobility, or to be foot soldiers in the army.

The working family was up by the time the sun rose. They ate a breakfast of cornmeal cooked in water like a porridge, and then flavored with chili peppers and possibly honey. The commoners wore simple clothing: the men had a loincloth, and a cape for cold weather. Women and girls had long skirts and blouses.

WOMEN WITH COLORFUL MAYA CLOTHING

The workers in the fields would have a mid-day meal of a cooked pastry filled with vegetables and meat. The family meal at the end of the day would usually be tortillas filled with vegetables and any meat or fish that was available. As the sun went down, the family would lie down on mats in their single room to go to sleep.

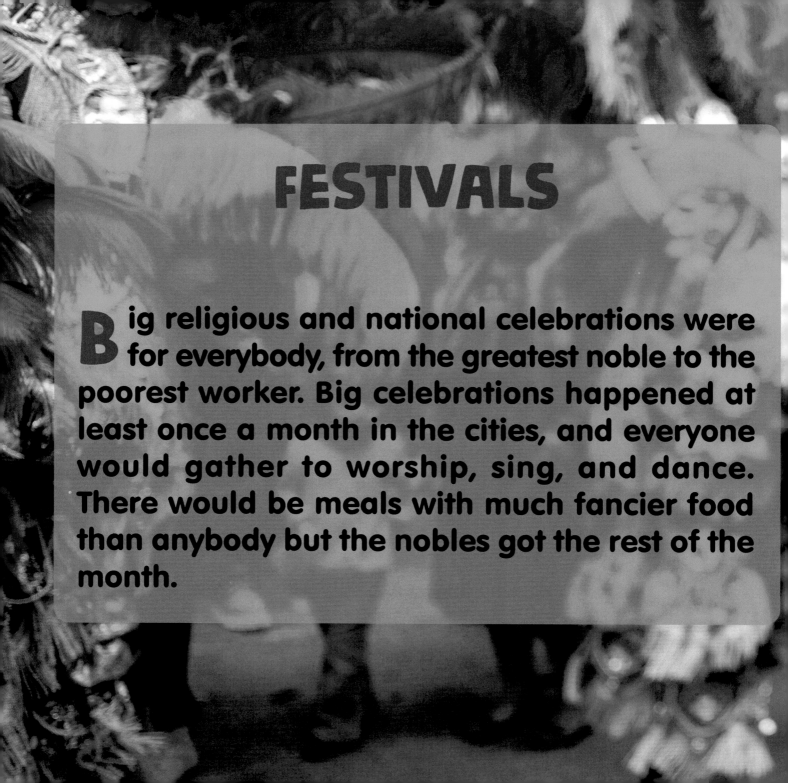

FESTIVALS

Big religious and national celebrations were for everybody, from the greatest noble to the poorest worker. Big celebrations happened at least once a month in the cities, and everyone would gather to worship, sing, and dance. There would be meals with much fancier food than anybody but the nobles got the rest of the month.

POK-A-TOK

One of the regular attractions of these events were sports competitions. One of the Mayan sports was Pok-a-Tok, which was played for fun and also to honor the gods. The game looked a little bit like basketball, with a court that had a goal at each end. The solid rubber ball weighed about five pounds, and players could not touch it with their hands or feet; but they could hit it with their upper arms or thighs to try to knock the ball through the goal.

FAMILY LIFE

At all levels of society, the Mayans usually lived in extended families with relatives from many generations in one house and under one roof. Usually families arranged marriages for their children, rather than waiting for the children to fall in love with somebody and decide to marry that person. The marriages helped to make a relationship between families so they would support each other in times of need.

FARMING

The main crops were corn, beans, and squash, usually all planted together in the same fields. They also raised peppers, sweet potatoes, tomatoes, papaya, onions, avocados, and garlic. Where the people grew fruit trees they would have access to pears and other fruit.

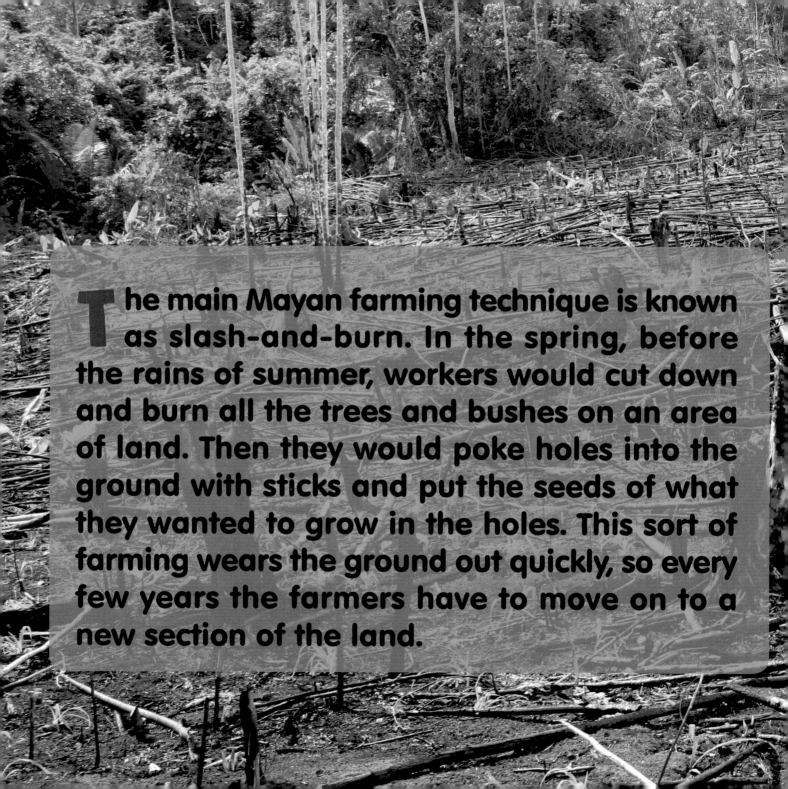

The main Mayan farming technique is known as slash-and-burn. In the spring, before the rains of summer, workers would cut down and burn all the trees and bushes on an area of land. Then they would poke holes into the ground with sticks and put the seeds of what they wanted to grow in the holes. This sort of farming wears the ground out quickly, so every few years the farmers have to move on to a new section of the land.

SLASH AND BURN CULTIVATION

FOLLOW THE MAYANS

What else can you find out about the Mayans and their world? These Baby Professor books can help you: A Quick History of the Mayan Civilization, The Mayans' Calendars and Advanced Writing System, The Mayans Gave us Their Art and Architecture, and The Mayan Cities.

Visit

BABY PROFESSOR
EDUCATION KIDS

www.BabyProfessorBooks.com

to download Free Baby Professor eBooks
and view our catalog of new and exciting
Children's Books

Made in the USA
Middletown, DE
09 April 2018